# America

## Come on a journey of discovery

Elaine Jackson

QED Publishing

**QED**

Copyright © QED Publishing 2004

First published in the UK by
QED Publishing
A division of Quarto Publishing plc
The Fitzpatrick Building
185-194 York Way, London N7 9QP

A Catalogue record for this book is available from
the British Library

ISBN 1 84538 057 6

Written by Elaine Jackson
with additional text by Ruth Urbom
Designed by Starry Dog Books Ltd
Edited by Christine Harvey
Map by PCGraphics (UK) Ltd

Creative Director: Louise Morley
Editorial Manager: Jean Coppendale

Picture credits

Key: t = top, b = bottom, m = middle, c = centre,
l = left, r = right

**Art Directors & TRIP** Eric Smith 6-7, / Adina Tovy
6ml, / Picturesque 8-9, / Anne-Marie Bazalik 9tl /
Viesti Associates 9tr, / Bob Turner 14-15, / Adina Tovy
18bl, / Tom Campbell 20-21, / Spencer Grant 21br, /
Adina Tovy 24-25, / Spencer Grant 26-27, / Martin
Barlow 26tr, / Adina Tovy 27tr;

**Corbis** Dean Conger 10bl, / Mark Peterson 10tr, /
Annie Griffith 12, / Nathan Benn 12tl, / David Muench
13tr, / Philip Gould 15tr, / Joseph Sohm 15tl, / Jim Sugar
18tr, / Gunter Marx 19, / John Van Hasselt 20tr, / Adam
Woolfit 23tl, / Larry Lee 23bl, / Mike Segar 25tl;

**Getty Images** Paul Souders 5tr, / David Young-Wolf
p11, / Gary Holscher 16bl, / Arthur Tilley 22

Printed and bound in China

The words in **bold** can
be found in the Glossary
on page 28.

# Contents

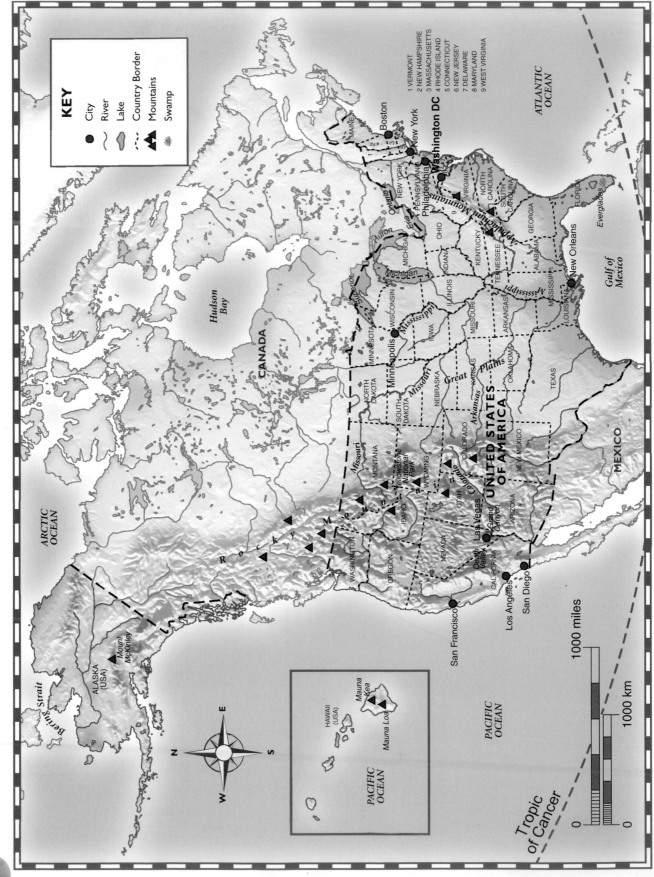

**KEY**

- City ●
- River 〜
- Lake
- Country Border - - -
- Mountains ▲
- Swamp ⚹

1 VERMONT
2 NEW HAMPSHIRE
3 MASSACHUSETTS
4 RHODE ISLAND
5 CONNECTICUT
6 NEW JERSEY
7 DELAWARE
8 MARYLAND
9 WEST VIRGINIA

ATLANTIC OCEAN

ARCTIC OCEAN

Hudson Bay

CANADA

MEXICO

UNITED STATES OF AMERICA

PACIFIC OCEAN

Gulf of Mexico

Bering Strait

Boston
New York
Washington DC
Philadelphia
New Orleans
Minneapolis
Las Vegas
Los Angeles
San Diego
San Francisco

MAINE
NEW YORK
PENNSYLVANIA
VIRGINIA
NORTH CAROLINA
SOUTH CAROLINA
GEORGIA
FLORIDA
OHIO
MICHIGAN
INDIANA
KENTUCKY
TENNESSEE
ALABAMA
MISSISSIPPI
LOUISIANA
WISCONSIN
ILLINOIS
IOWA
MISSOURI
ARKANSAS
MINNESOTA
NORTH DAKOTA
SOUTH DAKOTA
NEBRASKA
KANSAS
OKLAHOMA
TEXAS
MONTANA
WYOMING
COLORADO
NEW MEXICO
IDAHO
UTAH
ARIZONA
NEVADA
CALIFORNIA
OREGON
WASHINGTON

Appalachian Mountains

Rocky Mountains

Great Plains

Yellowstone National Park

Grand Canyon

Death Valley

Everglades

Superior
Huron
Michigan
Erie
Ontario

Mississippi
Missouri
Arkansas
Colorado

Mount McKinley

ALASKA (USA)

HAWAII (USA)
Mauna Kea
Mauna Loa
PACIFIC OCEAN

Tropic of Cancer

1000 miles
1000 km
0

N E S W

**4**

# Where in the world is the USA?

The United States of America (often called the USA) lies on the **continent** of North America. It is bordered on the west by the Pacific Ocean, on the east by the Atlantic Ocean and on the south by the Gulf of Mexico. The country to the north of the USA is Canada and to the south is Mexico.

The USA is the world's third largest country (after Russia and Canada). It has the world's third largest population (after China and India).

▼ The United States of America's place in the world.

the USA

▲ The national flag of the USA, often referred to as the 'Stars and Stripes'.

## Did you know?

**Name** United States of America
**Location** North America
**Surrounding countries** Canada and Mexico
**Surrounding oceans and seas** Atlantic Ocean, Pacific Ocean, Gulf of Mexico
**Length of coastline** 19 924km
**Capital city** Washington, DC
**Area** 9 809 000km$^2$
**Population** 290 342 554
**Life expectancy** Male 72, Female 79
**Religions** Christian 84% (Protestant 56%, Roman Catholic 28%), Jewish 2%
**Languages** English, Spanish also widely spoken
**Climate** Mostly **temperate** along the coasts, **tropical** in Hawaii and Florida, **arid** in the south-west, **arctic** in Alaska
**Highest mountain** Mount McKinley (also called Denali) in Alaska (6194m)
**Major rivers** Mississippi (length: 3779km), Missouri (length: 3726km), Arkansas (length: 2348km), Colorado (length: 2333km)
**Currency** US dollar. There are 100 cents in one dollar.

# What is the USA like?

## Travelling across the landscape

The USA consists of 50 states. As you travel through the USA, you will be amazed at the wide variety of landscapes. There are vast mountain ranges, huge flat grassy **plains**, hot deserts and frozen **glaciers**.

▼ A beach on Kauai, one of the islands of Hawaii.

## The south east

The southern coast along the Gulf of Mexico contains the great **delta** of the Mississippi River. If you travel here, you will see the **swamps** of the Everglades in Florida. This part of the USA is hit by more hurricanes than any other area.

## Central USA

The huge flat area known as the Great Plains is in the centre of the USA and extends westwards to the Rocky Mountains. Almost all the rivers and streams in the central part of the USA flow into the Mississippi–Missouri river system.

## The west

To the west of the Great Plains are the snow-capped Rocky Mountains. In the south of this region is the world's deepest valley, the Grand Canyon.

There is a fracture in the Earth's crust, running from San Francisco to Mexico, called the San Andreas Fault. The area around the San Andreas Fault suffers frequent earthquakes.

## Alaska and Hawaii

Alaska and Hawaii only became US states in 1959. They are separated from the rest of the USA and have very different climates and landscapes.

Alaska, in the extreme north west of North America, is an area of dramatic landscapes with glaciers and **fiords**.

Hawaii consists of a group of volcanic islands in the middle of the Pacific Ocean. Mauna Kea and Mauna Loa on the island of Hawaii are active volcanoes; the volcanoes on the other Hawaiian islands are no longer active. Hawaii has a **tropical** climate.

▲ The Majorie Glacier is situated in Glacier Bay, in Alaska. It sheds huge chunks of ice. This is known as 'calving'. Boat cruises to see the glacier are very popular.

## Did you know?

With its baking heat and burning sands, Death Valley in California has one of the most extreme climates on Earth. Badwater Basin in Death Valley is the lowest place in the western hemisphere. It is one of the hottest places in the entire world – temperatures there can reach 45° Celsius!

◄ The Grand Canyon, one of the world's most impressive scenic wonders, is located in the state of Arizona.

# Another State, another climate!

▼ Hurricanes and tornadoes can cause massive damage to houses and other buildings.

## A varied climate

As you travel around the USA, you will experience wide variations in the weather. The climate ranges from sizzling temperatures in the Californian desert to below freezing in Alaska.

## The western coastal states

Oregon and Washington, situated in the north west region along the Pacific coast, are among the wettest parts of the country. Temperatures here are mild all year round. Summers in California are generally dry, and inland areas can get very hot.

## The central states

The central areas of the USA are a long way from the sea. As a result their climates are more extreme. It can get extremely cold, with a lot of snow, in winter and then very hot in the summer. Severe thunderstorms cause heavy rain to fall on the Great Plains, accompanied by dangerous lightning and occasional tornadoes!

## The north east states

If you visit states such as Maine, Massachusetts and Pennsylvania, you will experience different weather at different times of the year. In winter, these areas experience heavy snow and freezing rain. Summers are usually sunny and warm, or even hot.

## The south east states

States such as Florida, Georgia and South Carolina experience moderate rains fairly evenly throughout the year. The winters are quite mild and short. Summers are hot and humid. Southern Florida usually has good weather all year round.

▼ Tornadoes can move quickly across the flat lands of the Great Plains.

## The south west states

States such as Arizona and New Mexico have the hottest temperatures in the USA. Unlike the south-east states, the climate here is very dry.

In January, Daniel is visiting his cousin in Colorado.

? What do you think the weather will be like? ?

? What sort of clothes should he pack? ?

? What sort of outdoor activities might they do? ?

# Eating across America

## Food origins

The food eaten in the USA is a mixture of native food and favourite meals brought to the country by **immigrants**. Recipes that the ancestors of today's Americans brought with them from their homelands are often passed down through families.

Although people across America eat many of the same foods, there are some that are more popular in certain areas. For example, fresh seafood is a great favourite in coastal areas.

Some types of foods and cooking are popular all across America. Mexican food, such as tacos and tortilla chips,

▼American families enjoy going out to eat together.

have been eaten throughout the USA for a long time. Chinese and Italian food are also common in every region.

## Eating out

Americans enjoy the convenience of eating in restaurants. Many people who travel to the USA are surprised by the huge size of the meals served in some American restaurants. But if you are unable to finish your meal in a family restaurant, you can ask for the left-overs to be put into a small container called a 'doggie bag', which you can take home with you. You don't have to give it to the dog though – you can finish the rest of your meal yourself later!

◄ People in New England enjoy eating fresh seafood.

Thanksgiving is on the fourth Thursday of November and dates back to 1621. When the Pilgrims came to America from England, about half of them died during their first winter. They turned to the Native Americans for help, and were taught how to plant crops. The next autumn's good harvest inspired the Pilgrims to give thanks by holding a feast. Foods eaten at that first Thanksgiving have become traditional and are still eaten today. All our family gathers together for Thanksgiving and we have a really special meal. We eat roast turkey, corn, sweet potatoes, cranberry sauce and pumpkin pie.

Amy wrote to her English pen friend about her family's Thanksgiving celebrations in the USA.

## Fast food

Fast-food restaurants that originated in America have spread all over the world. Many Americans like to grab a quick, tasty hamburger, hot dog or doughnut as they hurry from place to place in their busy lives.

▼ American families get together to enjoy a big Thanksgiving meal.

# The Mississippi River

## About the river

The name Mississippi comes from a Native American word meaning 'great waters'. The **source** of the mighty Mississippi is a number of very small streams in northern Minnesota. As the Mississippi flows southwards, it is joined by many **tributaries** including the Missouri River. The Mississippi forms part of the borders of ten different states.

Finally, the water flows into the Gulf of Mexico where it leaves behind the soil it has been carrying along. This soil forms a huge **delta.** The Mississippi river system is a busy shipping route and also provides a home for many kinds of wildlife.

▶ Traditional paddle-steamers on the Mississippi River in St Louis, Missouri.

▲ The Mississippi forms many small channels when it reaches its delta, where it flows into the Gulf of Mexico.

Dear Chloe
We took a steamboat tour along the Mississippi. The scenery was wonderful. Grandad enjoyed watching the trees and the wildlife along the river. The Mississippi is still important for transporting goods, and we saw lots of big barges passing by. The Mississippi is the world's third longest river system, after the Nile and the Amazon.
Love Nan and Grandad  x

Miss Chloe Jackson
Top House
Lees Lane
Little Neston
Cheshire
CH64 6AM
England

▲ Several small streams form the source of the Mississippi.

Chloe's grandparents are on holiday in the USA. They took a tour along the Mississippi in Louisiana on an old-fashioned paddlewheel steamboat. They sent postcards to Chloe, telling her about their adventures.

Dear Chloe
Here in the southern part of the USA, the Mississippi is over 1000m wide. The water flows slowly towards the Gulf of Mexico. It's hard to believe this huge river begins in Minnesota as just a small stream! It was so exciting to travel along part of it.
Love Nan and Grandad  x

Miss Chloe Jackson
Top House
Lees Lane
Little Neston
Cheshire
CH64 6AM
England

# The Great Lakes and Niagara Falls

## The Great Lakes

There are five Great Lakes. They are the world's largest group of freshwater lakes. One fifth of all the freshwater in the world lies in the four upper Great Lakes: Michigan, Huron, Superior and Erie. Their water is used for drinking and transport, as a source of power and for leisure activities.

▼ The natural beauty of Niagara Falls.

## Niagara Falls

Water flows from the four upper Great Lakes into the Niagara River. Then, at Niagara Falls, the water plunges 99 metres over a cliff. The sound of Niagara Falls is incredible, as the water spills over and crashes at the bottom. Niagara Falls is the second largest waterfall in the world. It stretches across the border between the USA and Canada. The water then travels 24 kilometres to the fifth Great Lake – Ontario. From Lake Ontario, the water enters the Saint Lawrence River and continues on to the Atlantic Ocean.

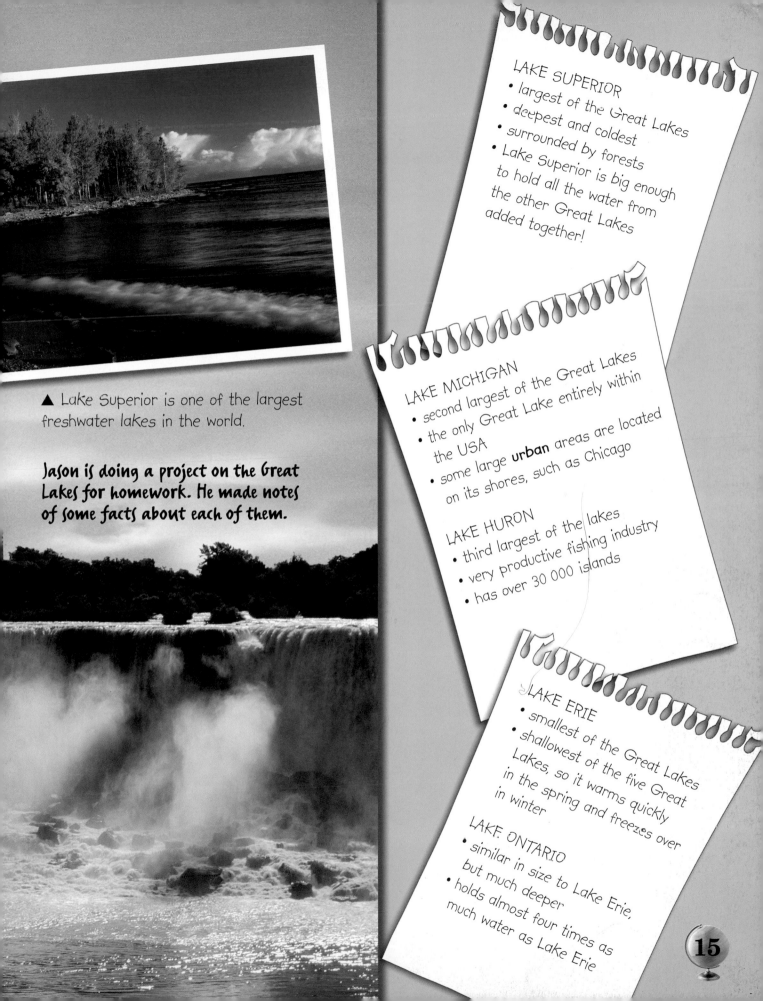

▲ Lake Superior is one of the largest freshwater lakes in the world.

Jason is doing a project on the Great Lakes for homework. He made notes of some facts about each of them.

**LAKE SUPERIOR**
- largest of the Great Lakes
- deepest and coldest
- surrounded by forests
- Lake Superior is big enough to hold all the water from the other Great Lakes added together!

**LAKE MICHIGAN**
- second largest of the Great Lakes
- the only Great Lake entirely within the USA
- some large **urban** areas are located on its shores, such as Chicago

**LAKE HURON**
- third largest of the lakes
- very productive fishing industry
- has over 30 000 islands

**LAKE ERIE**
- smallest of the Great Lakes
- shallowest of the five Great Lakes, so it warms quickly in the spring and freezes over in winter

**LAKE ONTARIO**
- similar in size to Lake Erie, but much deeper
- holds almost four times as much water as Lake Erie

# Travelling through the farming regions

The USA is the world's leading producer of food and provides for almost all its own food needs. It is the world's leading **exporter** of wheat and maize. It is also a major world producer of cheese, soya beans, tobacco, tomatoes, cattle (for beef), chickens, pigs, cotton and sugar.

▼ Wine is produced in California.

## Central USA

Travelling across the Great Plains, you will see large open areas of land with farms and ranches. Huge machines are used to plant and harvest the crops, such as wheat, which are grown in vast fields. Beef cattle are also raised throughout most of the Great Plains. Cattle ranching is especially important in Texas, where real cowboys still ride horses to do their work.

## Northern and eastern areas

The area around the Great Lakes is important for **dairy** farming. There are more dairy cows in the state of Wisconsin than in any other US state. Milk, cheese and other dairy products are produced in this region. New York and Vermont lead in the production of maple syrup.

▼ Fruit trees grow well in the north west of the country.

### The south east

As you travel on to the south east, you will see the tobacco-growing areas of North Carolina. Peanuts are produced in Georgia. Florida, with its tropical climate, is the USA's leading grower of oranges and other citrus fruits.

### California

California is America's leading producer of fruit and vegetables, such as lettuce, broccoli, strawberries and melons. A wide variety of produce is grown in the **fertile** soil of California's huge Central Valley.

California produces some of the world's greatest wines. The area has well-drained soil, warm days and cool nights, which are good conditions for wine grapes.

### The north west

The cooler climate of this region makes it suitable for growing fruits such as apples, pears, plums and cherries. The state of Idaho is famous for producing large amounts of potatoes.

▲ The Great Plains are nicknamed the 'breadbasket' of the USA.

# Tourism

## Visitor attractions

The USA has plenty to offer visitors from other countries. People travel to America to lie on sandy beaches and swim in the warm water off Florida's coasts, or to go skiing in the Rocky Mountains. There are historic places to visit, such as Boston in New England or Vicksburg on the Mississippi River. Not to mention the big-city excitement and shopping of New York or Los Angeles.

▼ The USA is famous for its theme parks, such as Disney World.

▲ The swampy wetlands of the Florida Everglades attract visitors keen to learn about the plants and wildlife there.

## Natural wonders

The USA has many natural attractions, including glaciers in Alaska, deserts in the south west and **geysers** in Wyoming. There are many national parks and forests where people can enjoy watching wild animals in their natural **habitats**. Yellowstone National Park, located in Idaho, Montana and Wyoming is the oldest park in the USA.

Hi Laura
I'm having a great time here in Florida. We went to Disney World yesterday, which was fantastic – there was just so much to do! I loved all the rides. We've spent a lot of time at the beach. The sun shines every day – no wonder they call it the Sunshine State!
I just don't want this holiday to end.
Bye for now,   Max

Laura Herbert
11 Marchbank Street
Little Frampton
Herefordshire
LF3 5ZZ
England

▼ Yellowstone National Park has thousands of hot springs and natural geysers, including the world famous Old Faithful geyser, which shoots out a jet of water approximately every hour.

# Industry and education

▼ The Coca Cola Company is famous throughout the world. There is even a museum in Atlanta dedicated to it.

## More than one type of power

During the 20th century, the USA became the richest and most powerful country in the world. It has vast resources, including deposits of iron ore and oil. The country's huge energy needs are met by its natural resources, such as **hydro-electric power**, as well as electricity produced from coal, oil and nuclear power.

## Working in the USA

Most American people have a very high standard of living. Unemployment is low and highly educated workers can earn good salaries. About three quarters of the population work in service industries, such as **retail**, banking, insurance, health care, teaching and tourism.

## Industry

American scientists have a long history of making technological advances in many fields. In 1969, US scientists built the first spaceship to take people to the moon and back. Today, the USA leads the world in computer technology and in developing medical, **aerospace** and military equipment.

America's aluminium, steel and car **industries** are among the biggest in the world. The USA exports **raw materials** such as cotton, iron and chemical products around the world.

Other major American industries include publishing, films, food processing, **telecommunications** and paper making.

▼ Hydro-electric power is provided by the Hoover Dam on the border between Arizona and Nevada.

## Education

Children enter kindergarten, the first year of school, at age 5. Each autumn they begin a new grade. Elementary school consists of the first six numbered grades, where children stay until the age of about 12. Secondary education is usually divided into junior high school (grades 7–9) and senior high school (grades 10–12). After graduating from high school, over 60 per cent of students continue their education at a college or university. There are over 3000 universities and colleges in the USA.

▼ American scientists conduct important new research.

# The nation's capital

▶ The US President lives and works in the White House.

Washington, DC is America's capital city. The letters DC stand for 'District of Columbia', which is the official title for the area where the city of Washington is located. It is not actually located within any of the 50 US states. When Washington was chosen to become America's national capital, it was thought that it would be unfair if any one state received the honour of being the location of the national government.

Washington, DC is named after George Washington, who was the first President of the USA. Before he was elected as President, George Washington was famous as an army general in America's war of independence from Britain.

## The seat of government

America's President and Vice-President both live and work in Washington. The President lives in the White House, which also contains his office (known as the Oval Office because of its shape), as well as offices for his staff.

The US Congress, America's national law-making organization, meets in the US Capitol Building in Washington.

There are two houses of Congress to which members are elected: the Senate and the House of Representatives.

America's highest court, the US Supreme Court, and many other government departments are also located in Washington.

◄ The US Capitol Building houses the offices and meeting chambers of the Senate and the House of Representatives.

► The Lincoln Memorial in Washington, DC honours President Abraham Lincoln, who is remembered for freeing the American slaves in the 1860s.

## Did you know?

In Washington's many museums you can see important objects from significant historical events. For example, at the National Air and Space Museum you can see the plane that made the world's first successful flight in 1903, as well as part of the spacecraft that carried the first astronauts to walk on the moon in 1969.

## Amazing, but true!

When it was built in 1800, the White House was the largest house in the entire USA.

In 1814, the White House and the Capitol Building were partially burnt down by British soldiers.

The White House has its own swimming pool, bowling alley and cinema for the President and his family.

# New York, New York!

► The Statue of Liberty is the USA's symbol of freedom.

### Where is New York?

There are actually two places called New York: New York City and New York State. New York City, or the 'Big Apple' as it is sometimes called, lies at the mouth of the Hudson River. Even though New York City is by far the largest city in New York State, it is not the state capital. The state government is located in the capital city of Albany.

### Manhattan

The first Europeans to settle on Manhattan Island in the 1620s were the Dutch. They called the city New Amsterdam. In 1664, the British took over and renamed it New York. Manhattan is now one of the five boroughs at the heart of this huge city.

### A multi-cultural city

Since the early days of the USA, New York has been a place where people from all over the world have come to start new lives in America. As a result, most of the languages of the world are spoken by New York's multi-cultural inhabitants.

◀ The New York Knicks are a popular basketball team. They play in orange, blue and white - the official colours of New York City.

**Josh decided to write an article about New York City for his class travel brochure.**

▼ New York has many huge skyscrapers.

A visit to the observation room on the 102nd floor of the Empire State Building will allow you to see breathtaking views over New York.

After this, take a trip on the Staten Island Ferry to see the Statue of Liberty. Then move on to the hustle and bustle of Times Square. Broadway and 42nd Street, famous for their theatres and restaurants, meet here. The city also has lots of museums and great shopping streets.

If, after all this excitement, you are finding the streets hot and stuffy, Central Park offers the biggest green space in the city. Here you can stroll through the park or take part in activities such as pony riding, tennis or skating.

# Travelling to California and the West coast cities

## About California

California is the third largest state in the USA. Its nickname is the 'Golden State'. In 1849, thousands of people rushed to California in search of gold after it was discovered there. Today, California has the highest population of any state in the USA.

▶ In San Francisco, cable cars rattle around the city's hilly streets.

SAN FRANCISCO
This is one of the USA's most unusual cities. San Francisco has a wonderful harbour and bay. It has famous bridges, such as the Golden Gate Bridge. The San Francisco area sometimes has earthquakes, so buildings are built to be 'earthquake proof'.

By Katie

Josh's friends decided to find out about cities on the west coast for their class travel brochure.

HOLLYW

**LOS ANGELES**
This is a huge sprawling city. Its attractions include Beverly Hills, famous for its exclusive shopping, and the theme parks of Universal Studios and Disneyland. Hollywood is actually part of the city of Los Angeles. Films have been made in Hollywood since 1911.

By Emma

**SAN DIEGO**
San Diego is located near California's border with Mexico. The weather is usually warm and sunny. San Diego has miles of beaches, world-class sailing, great museums and the world's largest zoo.

By Steve

▼ Las Vegas is in the Nevada desert. The flashy casinos light up the streets at night.

**LAS VEGAS**
Las Vegas, in Nevada, is a fun city for grown-ups. With many neon lights, it is a city that never sleeps. Some people visit the city to get married. Others enjoy visiting its many casinos, restaurants and shopping malls. The casinos stay open 24 hours a day, 7 days a week!

By Laura

◄ Hollywood is the centre of America's film industry.

27

# Glossary

**aerospace**
companies involved in building planes and spacecraft

**arctic**
an arctic climate is very cold, with a lot of snow

**arid**
very dry, with almost no rain

**continent**
one of the seven large areas of land on the Earth's surface: Africa, Asia, Australia, Antarctica, North America, South America and Europe

**dairy**
a place where cows' milk is taken and made into other food products

**delta**
an area at the mouth of a large river where the river flows into the sea

**exports**
goods sold to other countries

**fertile**
able to grow or produce a lot of things

**fiord**
a narrow area of sea that has tall rocky cliffs along its sides

**geyser**
a natural hot spring which shoots a jet of hot water into the air

**glacier**
a huge mass of ice that moves slowly across the land

**habitat**
a natural area where animals live

**hydro-electric power**
electricity made from the controlled flow of water

**immigrants**
people who have come to live in a new country

**industry**
what a country makes, for example, in factories or workshops

**plain**
a large area of low, flat land

**raw materials**
things such as iron or coal that are used for making other goods

**retail**
selling things in shops and stores

**source**
where a river or stream starts

**swamp**
an area of low-lying land which is permanently wet

**telecommunications**
telephones and the wires and networks for connecting them

**temperate**
a temperate climate is not too hot or too cold

**tributary**
a river or stream that flows into another, often larger, one

**tropical**
a tropical climate is hot and rainy

**urban**
located in a large town or city

# Index

# Teaching ideas and activities for children

The following activities address and develop the geographical 'enquiry' approach, and promote thinking skills and creativity. The activities in section A have been devised to help children develop higher order thinking, based on Bloom's taxonomy of thinking. The activities in section B have been devised to promote different types of learning styles, based on Howard Gardner's theory of multiple intelligences.

## A: ACTIVITIES TO DEVELOP THINKING SKILLS

### ACTIVITIES TO PROMOTE RESEARCH AND RECALL OF FACTS

*Ask the children to:*

• make an alphabet book for a young child, illustrating the contrasts in the USA (for example, physical features, weather, industry).
• research and investigate a mountain environment (the Rocky Mountains) or a tropical swamp area (the Everglades in Florida). The children could present their information in a poster or a Powerpoint presentation.

### ACTIVITIES TO PROMOTE UNDERSTANDING

*Ask the children to:*

• replicate a simple A3 map or picture of America. Place the children in groups of four to six. Tell them they are going to reproduce the map or picture you have provided. In their groups, ask them to number themselves and to discuss strategies they could use to reproduce your picture. Call each number, one at a time, to look at the picture for two minutes. Then ask them to go back and draw what they can remember, while discussing the picture and strategies with their group. Give the children five minutes to do this. Then call the next member of the group, and so on. At the end, show the children the original and ask them to evaluate each group's work.
• make a flow chart to show 'A year in the life of a cotton plant' or 'The production of corn (maize)'.

## ACTIVITIES TO PROMOTE THE USE OF KNOWLEDGE AND SKILLS TO SOLVE PROBLEMS

*Ask the children to:*

• make notes to explain the reasons why the streets in New York are so busy and congested.

• produce a poster, in groups, advertising different types of holidays to the USA, such as a skiing trip to the Rocky Mountains or a visit to Disney World.

## ACTIVITIES TO ENCOURAGE ANALYTICAL THINKING

*Ask the children to:*

• compare and contrast life in New York with life in a city in the UK.

• use reference books and the Internet to write a journalistic report about an earthquake in California or a tornado on the south coast.

## ACTIVITIES TO PROMOTE CREATIVITY

*Ask the children to:*

• make a representation of the Everglades in Florida or the Grand Canyon, using collage or painting.

• design a word search, including geographical words.

## ACTIVITIES TO HELP CHILDREN USE EVIDENCE TO FORM OPINIONS AND EVALUATE CONSEQUENCES OF DECISIONS

*Ask the children to:*

• rank five of the places in this book in order of preference, giving reasons why they would like to visit them.

• in pairs, decide on five items that would best represent life in the USA. Encourage the children to explain the reasons behind their choices.

# B: ACTIVITIES BASED ON DIFFERENT LEARNING STYLES

## ACTIVITIES FOR LINGUISTIC LEARNERS

*Ask the children to:*

• write a rap to promote New York as a great place for a holiday.

• write a journalistic report about living in the 'Big Apple'.

## ACTIVITIES FOR LOGICAL AND MATHEMATICAL LEARNERS

Ask the children to use the Internet to find out about the climate in Florida and Alaska, and to represent the differences graphically.

## ACTIVITIES FOR VISUAL LEARNERS

*Ask the children to:*
- locate the major cities and rivers on a map of the USA.
- draw their favourite place in the USA on a postcard-sized piece of card.

## ACTIVITIES FOR KINAESTHETIC LEARNERS

*Ask the children to:*
- make some muffins (with adult support).
- make a model of a volcanic eruption on Mauna Loa or Mauna Kea.
- enact the eruption of a volcano, using dance and drama.

## ACTIVITIES FOR MUSICAL LEARNERS

Ask the children to create and perform a simple country and western or jazz tune, using available instruments.

## ACTIVITIES FOR INTER-PERSONAL LEARNERS

Ask the children to plan a holiday itinerary for a visit to the USA for their family.

## ACTIVITIES FOR INTRA-PERSONAL LEARNERS

Ask the children to describe how they would feel looking across New York from the 102nd floor of the Empire State Building, or flying over the Grand Canyon.

## ACTIVITIES FOR NATURALISTIC LEARNERS

Ask the children to make notes and prepare a speech for a debate on either the pros or the cons of maintaining the national parks and/or wilderness areas in the USA.

# LINKS ACROSS THE CURRICULUM

The **Travel Through** series of books offers up-to-date information and cross-curricular opportunities for teaching geography, literacy, numeracy, history, RE, PSHE and citizenship. The series enables children to develop an overview ('the big picture') of each country. This overview reflects the huge diversity and richness of the life and culture of each country. The series aims to prevent the development of misconceptions, stereotypical images and prejudices, which often develop when the focus of a study narrows too quickly onto a small locality within a country. The books in the series help children not only to gain access to this overview, but to develop an understanding of how places are connected. They contribute to the children's geographical knowledge, skills and understanding, and help the children to make sense of the world around them.